THE CASE FOR
Faith

—

STUDY GUIDE
Revised Edition

Resources by Lee Strobel

The Case for Christ

The Case for Christ audio

The Case for Christ Student Edition (with Jane Vogel)

The Case for Christ curriculum (with Garry Poole)

The Case for Christmas

The Case for Christmas audio

The Case for a Creator

The Case for a Creator audio

The Case for Creator Student Edition (with Jane Vogel)

The Case for a Creator curriculum (with Garry Poole)

The Case for Easter

The Case for Faith

The Case for Faith audio

The Case for Faith Student Edition (with Jane Vogel)

The Case for Faith curriculum (with Garry Poole)

The Case for the Real Jesus

The Case for the Real Jesus audio

Faith Under Fire curriculum

God's Outrageous Claims

Inside the Mind of Unchurched Harry and Mary

Off My Case for Kids

Surviving a Spiritual Mismatch in Marriage (with Leslie Strobel)

Surviving a Spiritual Mismatch in Marriage audio

What Jesus Would Say

Other Resources by Garry Poole

The Complete Book of Questions

Seeker Small Groups

In the Tough Questions Series:

Don't All Religions Lead to God?

How Could God Allow Suffering and Evil?

How Does Anyone Know God Exists?

Why Become a Christian?

Tough Questions Leader's Guide (with Judson Poling)

THE CASE FOR

Faith

—

Investigating the
Toughest Objections to Christianity

LEE
STROBEL

NEW YORK TIMES BESTSELLING AUTHOR

AND GARRY POOLE

Revised Edition

Willow Creek Resources

ZONDERVAN

The Case for Faith Study Guide Revised Edition
Copyright © 2008, 2013 by Lee Strobel and Garry Poole

This title is also available as a Zondervan ebook. Visit www.zondervan.com/ebooks.

Requests for information should be addressed to:

Zondervan, *Grand Rapids, Michigan 49530*

ISBN 978-0-310-69880-7

Cover design: Faceout Studio
Cover photography: Shutterstock®
Interior design: Beth Shagene

Printed in the United States of America

13 14 15 16 17 18 19 20 /DCI/ 23 22 21 20 19 18 17 16 15 14 13 12 11 10 9 8 7 6 5 4 3 2 1

Contents

*Special thanks to
Laura Allen and Jim Poole
for their outstanding writing and editing contributions.
Their creative insights and suggestions
took this guide to the next level.*

The Challenge of Faith

For me, having lived much of my life as an atheist, the last thing I want is a naive faith built on a paper-thin foundation of wishful thinking or make-believe. I need a faith that's consistent with reason, not contradictory to it; I want beliefs that are grounded in reality, not detached from it. I need to find out once and for all whether the Christian faith can stand up to scrutiny. It was time for me to talk face to face with Charles Templeton.

Lee Strobel, *The Case for Faith*

Read This!

If possible, read the introduction ("The Challenge of Faith") and "On the Road to Answers" in *The Case for Faith* book in preparation for your group meeting. Otherwise, read it as follow-up.

Watch This!

Video Teaching Segment

Space is provided to take notes on anything that stands out to you.

Discuss This!

1. What are your greatest doubts in life? What spiritual doubts do you carry around with you?

> *"Reason and faith are opposites, two mutually exclusive terms: there is no reconciliation or common ground. Faith is belief without, or in spite of, reason."*
> — Atheist George H. Smith

THINK ABOUT THIS!

"All of us want somebody to love us. Well, I want to tell you that God loves you. He loves you so much that he gave us his Son to die on the cross for our sins. And he loves you so much that he will come into your life and change the direction of your life and make you a new person, whoever you are."

Billy Graham

"What is faith? There would have been no need to define it for these people listening to Billy Graham preach on that sultry June night. Faith was almost palpable to them. They reached out to God almost as if they were expecting to physically embrace him. Faith drained them of the guilt that had oppressed them. Faith replaced despondency with hope. Faith infused them with new direction and purpose. Faith unlocked heaven. Faith was like cool water soaking their parched soul."

Lee Strobel

"But faith isn't always that easy, even for people who desperately want it. Some people hunger for spiritual certainty, yet something hinders them from experiencing it. They wish they could taste that kind of freedom, but obstacles block their paths. Objections pester them. Doubts mock them. Their hearts want to soar to God; their intellects keep them securely tied down."

Lee Strobel

> "I had preached to hundreds of thousands of people the antithetical message, and then I found to my dismay that I could no longer believe it. To believe it would be to deny the brain I had been given. It became quite clear that I had been wrong."
>
> Charles Templeton

2. How do you define doubt? Where do doubts come from? What effect do they have on people when they hit? What are the pros and cons of a healthy dose of doubt?

_____

"Faith is a rational response to the evidence of God's self-revelation in nature, human history, the Scriptures and his resurrected Son."
— Christian educator W. Bingham Hunter

3. Briefly describe your faith journey. When have you been closest to God on your journey in life and at what points have you felt furthest away from him? Explain.

THINK ABOUT THIS!

*"If a person has faith and it makes them a better individual, then I'm all for that —
even if I think they're nuts. Having been a Christian, I know how important it is to
people's lives — how it alters their decisions, how it helps them deal with difficult
problems. For most people, it's a boon beyond description. But is it because there is
a God? No, it's not."*

Charles Templeton

*"Is that what faith is all about — fooling yourself into becoming a better person?
Convincing yourself there's a God so that you'll become motivated to ratchet up your
morality a notch or two? Embracing a fairy tale so you'll sleep better at night? No
thank you, I thought to myself. If that's faith, I wasn't interested."*

Lee Strobel

4. To what extent are questions and doubts regarding spiritual matters inevitable? Why? Is faith a simple process of belief or does it require a certain degree of thought and struggle or a combination of both? Explain.

THINK ABOUT THIS!

*"I had gone through a conversion experience as an incredibly green youth. I lacked
the intellectual skills and the theological training needed to buttress my beliefs
when — as was inevitable — questions and doubts began to plague me … My reason
had begun to challenge and sometimes to rebut the central beliefs of the Christian
faith."*

Charles Templeton

"Father, I am going to accept this as Thy Word — by faith! I'm going to allow faith to go beyond my intellectual questions and doubts, and I will believe this to be Your inspired Word."

Billy Graham

5. Why do you think Charles Templeton abandoned the faith that had once been the cornerstone of his life?

THINK ABOUT THIS!

"Christian theism must be rejected by any person with even a shred of respect for reason."

George H. Smith, atheist

"Christian faith is not an irrational leap. Examined objectively, the claims of the Bible are rational propositions well supported by reason and evidence."

Charles Colson, Christian

6. Does the process of asking tough spiritual questions ruin or strengthen one's faith? Why? If you could ask God one question and you knew he would answer you right away, what would it be?

THINK ABOUT THIS!

Now faith is confidence in what we hope for and assurance about what we do not see.

Hebrews 11:1

We live by faith, not by sight.

2 Corinthians 5:7

Jesus said to the woman, "Your faith has saved you; go in peace."

Luke 7:50

For it is by grace you have been saved, through faith — and this not from yourselves, it is the gift of God.

Ephesians 2:8

In all this you greatly rejoice, though now for a little while you may have had to suffer grief in all kinds of trials. These have come so that proven genuineness of your faith — of greater worth than gold, which perishes even though refined by fire — may result in praise, glory and honor when Jesus Christ is revealed. Though you have not seen him, you love him; and even though you do not see him now, you believe in him and are filled with an inexpressible and glorious joy, for you are receiving the end result of your faith, the salvation of your souls.

1 Peter 1:6 – 9

7. How does society define faith? According to the preceding Bible verses (see the "Think About This!" box), how does the Bible define it? Why does God place so much emphasis on faith?

8. Lee suggests that the process of asking tough spiritual questions is crucial because the answers we find inevitably influence our perceptions of God. Do you agree or disagree with Lee's reasoning? In what ways do the answers we obtain shape, and even distort, our perceptions of the truth?

9. Is it unfair of God to require faith of us when there are so many obstacles to overcome in order to have it? Is God too demanding? Does he require "blind faith"? Give reasons for your responses.

THINK ABOUT THIS!

"The atheist says there is no God. The Christian and Jew say there is a God. The agnostic says, 'I cannot know.' Not 'do not know' but 'cannot know.' I never would presume to say flatly that there is no God. I don't know everything; I'm not the embodiment of wisdom. But it is not possible for me to believe in God.

"I have spent a lifetime thinking about it. If this were a simplistic conclusion reached on a whim, that would be different. But it's impossible for me — impossible — to believe that there is any thing or person or being that could be described as a loving God who could allow what happens in our world daily."

Charles Templeton

"Jesus was the greatest human being who has ever lived. He was a moral genius. His ethical sense was unique. He was the intrinsically wisest person that I've ever encountered in my life or in my readings. His commitment was total and led to his own death, much to the detriment of the world. What could one say about him except that this was a form of greatness?

"In my view he is the most important human being who has ever existed. And if I may put it this way, I ... miss ... him!"

Charles Templeton

OPTIONAL DISCUSSION QUESTIONS
for Those Investigating Christianity

• Describe the genesis of your doubt about God—how and why did it begin? Why does it sometimes seem so complicated or difficult to believe in God?

• What kinds of questions have challenged your ability to believe in the validity of the Bible, the deity of Jesus, or the existence of God?

• According to Lee's interview, Templeton wasn't looking for a response regarding his troubling issues so much as he wanted to be understood. To what degree do you just want your doubts to be understood?

• In Templeton's case, the process of reasoning had chased away his faith. But are faith and intellect really incompatible? Is it possible to be a "thinker" and a follower of Jesus at the same time? Explain.

• Are Christian beliefs deleterious to individuals and to society as Charles Templeton has stated?

• Describe your stance regarding the existence of God. Do you consider yourself more of an agnostic, an atheist, a believer in God, or some other category?

Between Sessions

Personal Reflection

> *People were bringing little children to Jesus for him to place his hands*
> *on them, but the disciples rebuked them. When Jesus saw this, he was*
> *indignant. He said to them, "Let the little children come to me, and*
> *do not hinder them, for the kingdom of God belongs to such as these.*
> *Truly I tell you, anyone who will not receive the kingdom of God like*
> *a little child will never enter it."*
>
> (Mark 10:13–15)

1. What is it about little children that makes them so absolutely trusting? How often do you long for the faith of a child when it comes to spiritual matters and life in general? Aren't things just simpler for those who believe things easily and never second-guess what they've been told?

2. Then again, isn't it those who trust easily who get taken advantage of? What is it about giving away trust that makes you vulnerable to disappointment, rejection, and hurt? How many times have you been let down by the very ones you thought would be there for you, the very ones who promised to take care of you? How many times have you said, "Never again"?

3. Little children flocked to Jesus, and he welcomed them and loved each one unconditionally. What did Jesus demonstrate to his followers about his trustworthiness when he welcomed and embraced the little children? What is it about Jesus that makes him so different and so completely worthy of such unabashed faith? And what is it about faith in God that is so alluring and yet at times so difficult?

4. The Bible tells us that Jesus was also completely pure and innocent — completely sinless — making him the *only one* absolutely worthy of our complete trust. Do you believe this? How might your life be different if you were able to begin to trust God with renewed faith?

Personal Reading

Please read the following book content in preparation for session two:

The Case for Faith, Objection #8: I Still Have Doubts, So I Can't Be a Christian

Dealing
with Doubts

Scholars have wrestled with these issues for years, but I didn't want to talk with some professor whose interest in doubt was merely antiseptic and academic. I wanted to get answers from someone who has personally known the confusion, the guilt, the maddening ambiguity of uncertainty — and that lured me to Dallas to interview a Christian leader whose faith journey has repeatedly taken him on torturous detours through the valley of the shadow of doubt.

Lee Strobel, *The Case for Faith*

Watch This!

Video Teaching Segment

Space is provided to take notes on anything that stands out to you.

Discuss This!

1. Some people find faith in God without much struggle and others have a tendency to wrestle with nagging doubts. How are you wired? Do you have a propensity toward faith or a propensity toward doubt?

THINK ABOUT THIS!

"I knew that misconceptions about faith often open the door to doubts because they can create false expectations or misunderstandings about the nature of God. For instance, if people incorrectly think God has promised to heal everyone or make everyone wealthy if they just exhibit sufficient faith, they can fall prey to doubts when illness strikes or bankruptcy looms."

Lynn Anderson

2. Lynn Anderson warns that it's possible to define God in ways that set up disappointment and disillusionment. How does your current view of God affect your expectations of him?

3. Have your expectations regarding God's promises ever caused your faith to falter? For example, have you ever prayed sincerely for something very important to you and seemingly gotten no answer? If so, how did you feel about it? How did you react? How has this apparent lack of response from God affected your view of him?

4. Anderson claims that we will always encounter challenges to our faith because we will never have all the answers. If this is true, how is it possible for faith to survive? If doubt detracts from faith, how is it possible for anyone to ever have hope and certainty about anything? Why do you think God seems to leave so many important questions unanswered?

"In their most inner thoughts, even the most devout Christians know that there is something illegitimate about belief. Underneath their profession of faith is a sleeping giant of doubt … In my experience, the best way to conquer doubt is to yield to it."
— Dan Barker, pastor-turned-atheist

THINK ABOUT THIS!

"You unbelieving generation," Jesus replied, "how long shall I stay with you? How long shall I put up with you? Bring the boy to me." So they brought him. When the spirit saw Jesus, it immediately threw the boy into a convulsion. He fell to the ground and rolled around, foaming at the mouth. Jesus asked the boy's father, "How long has he been like this?" "From childhood," he answered. "It has often thrown him into fire or water to kill him. But if you can do anything, take pity on us and help us." " 'If you can'?" said Jesus. "Everything is possible for one who believes." Immediately the boy's father exclaimed, "I do believe; help me overcome my unbelief!"

Mark 9:19 – 24

"Yes, some people think that faith means a lack of doubt, but that's not true. One of my favorite Bible texts is about the man who comes to Jesus with his demon-possessed son, hoping that the boy would get healed. Jesus says all things are possible to those who believe. And the man's response is so powerful. He says, 'I believe, but would you help me with my unbelief?'"

Lynn Anderson

5. In the Mark 9 passage, a man cries to Jesus, "I do believe, help me overcome my unbelief!" How is it possible to believe and yet not believe? To what degree can you relate to this man? Which aspects of Christianity are easier for you to believe than others?

THINK ABOUT THIS!

"There was another important implication of Anderson's interview. If doubt and faith can coexist, then this means people don't have to fully resolve each and every obstacle between them and God in order to have an authentic faith. In other words, when the preponderance of all the evidence tilts decisively in God's favor, and a person then makes the rational choice to put their trust in him, they can hold some

of their more peripheral objections in tension until the day comes when they're re-
solved. In the meantime, they can still make the choice to believe—and ask God to
help them with their unbelief."

Lee Strobel

6. Do people need to resolve every one of their questions before they can make a relational decision to follow Jesus? Can a person be a Christian and nevertheless have reservations or doubts? If Jesus were to prove himself trustworthy in ways that are verifiable, how much more willing would you be to trust him in areas you cannot verify? Give reasons for your responses.

THINK ABOUT THIS!

"For many Christians, merely having doubts of any kind can be scary. They wonder
whether their questions disqualify them being a follower of Christ. They feel insecure
because they're not sure whether it's permissible to express uncertainty about God,
Jesus, or the Bible. So they keep their questions to themselves—and inside, unan-
swered, they grow and fester and loom until they eventually succeed in choking out
their faith."

Lee Strobel

[Jesus] replied, "If you have faith as small as a mustard seed, you can say to this mulberry tree, 'Be uprooted and planted in the sea,' and it will obey you."

Luke 17:6

"It's not the amount of faith you can muster that matters up front. It may be tiny, like a mustard seed. But your faith must be invested in something solid. So people need to clarify their reasons for believing. Why should they believe in Jesus rather than the Maharishi? Why do they believe in crystals or in Oriental mysticism? Where's the substance? Obviously, I'm prejudiced but when it comes right down to it, the only object of faith that is solidly supported by the evidence of history and archaeology and literature and experience is Jesus."

Lynn Anderson

7. Which faith do you think is stronger: blind faith that avoids doubt, or examined faith that faces challenges? In what ways is faith strengthened by adversity? How is the process of struggling with doubts and questions able to draw one closer to God in the long run?

"We like to focus on the upbeat Psalms, but 60 percent of them are laments, with people screaming out, 'God, where are you?' Normal faith is allowed to beat on God's chest and complain."
— Lynn Anderson

THINK ABOUT THIS!

"The shame is not that people have doubts, but that they are ashamed of them."

Os Guinness

"Those who believe they believe in God but without passion in the heart, without anguish of mind, without uncertainty, without doubt, and even at times without despair, believe only in the idea of God, and not in God himself."

Madeleine L'Engle

"If faith never encounters doubt, if truth never struggles with error, if good never battles with evil, how can faith know its own power? In my own pilgrimage, if I have to choose between a faith that has stared doubt in the eye and made it blink, or a naive faith that has never known the firing line of doubt, I will choose the former every time."

Gary Parker

"The struggle with God is not lack of faith — it is faith!"

André Resner

"I always get a little nervous at what I call the 'true believer' mentality — people with bright smiles and glassy eyes who never have a doubt in the world, who always think everything's wonderful, everything's great. I don't think they run in the same world I do. I'm afraid of what's going to happen to them when something bad occurs."

Lynn Anderson

8. Read the following Bible excerpts depicting various struggles people had with God.

> *How long, O LORD, must I call for help? But you do not listen! "Violence is everywhere!" I cry, but you do not come to save. Must I forever see these evil deeds? Why must I watch all this misery? Wherever I look, I see destruction and violence. I am surrounded by people who love to argue and fight. The law has become paralyzed, and there is no justice in the courts. The wicked far outnumber the righteous, so that justice has become perverted.*
>
> Habakkuk 1:2–4 NLT

> *At last Job spoke, and he cursed the day of his birth. He said: "Let the day of my birth be erased, and the night I was conceived. Let that*

day be turned to darkness. Let it be lost even to God on high, and let no light shine on it. Let the darkness and utter gloom claim that day for its own. Let a black cloud overshadow it, and let the darkness terrify it. Let that night be blotted off the calendar, never again to be counted among the days of the year, never again to appear among the months. Let that night be childless. Let it have no joy. Let those who are experts at cursing — whose cursing could rouse Leviathan — curse that day. Let its morning stars remain dark. Let it hope for light, but in vain; may it never see the morning light. Curse that day for failing to shut my mother's womb, for letting me be born to see all this trouble.

Job 3:1 – 10 NLT

Hear my voice when I call, LORD; be merciful to me and answer me. My heart says of you, "Seek his face!" Your face, LORD, I will seek. Do not hide your face from me, do not turn your servant away in anger; you have been my helper. Do not reject me or forsake me, God my Savior. Though my father and mother forsake me, the LORD will receive me. Teach me your way, LORD; lead me in a straight path because of my oppressors. Do not turn me over to the desire of my foes, for false witnesses rise up against me, spouting malicious accusations. I remain confident of this: I will see the goodness of the LORD in the land of the living.

Psalm 27:7 – 13

Note that each of these people had great faith in God and yet were honest with their objections, fears, and doubts. In return, God respected, honored, and often answered their heartfelt pleas. How do these honest conversations with God impact you? Why do you think these examples are included in the Bible?

THINK ABOUT THIS!

"In the gospel of John, faith is never a noun, it's always a verb. Faith is action; it's never just mental assent. It's a direction of life. So when we begin to do faith, God begins to validate it. And the further we follow the journey, the more we know it's true."

Lynn Anderson

Taste and see that the LORD is good.

Psalm 34:8

9. How does one begin to "do faith" as Lynn Anderson suggests? And what does it mean to "taste and see that the LORD is good"? What makes it possible to take a step of faith and choose to trust God even in the face of doubt?

As the heavens are higher than the earth,
so are my ways higher than your ways
and my thoughts than your thoughts.

— Isaiah 55:9

OPTIONAL DISCUSSION QUESTIONS
for Those Investigating Christianity

- How much doubt can a person have before he or she no longer believes? Explain. How much doubt are you personally able to tolerate and yet still believe in Jesus and the claims of the Bible?

- How often does your mind gravitate to questions for which there are no answers? Why do you think that is?

- Is doubt a part of the universal human experience and, if so, what is its function?

- Does having faith mean the removal of all doubt (in other words, 100 percent certainty)? What is the significance behind Jesus' analogy in comparing the tiniest of seeds with one's level of faith?

- Why would it matter more *where* one's faith is invested than the *amount* of faith one demonstrates? What is the distinction between these two concepts?

- When, if ever, is it okay to complain to God or even argue with him?

- Can we ever know everything there is to know about why God allows what happens in this world? How much is possible to comprehend? To what degree is God, by definition, impossible to understand fully?

- In what ways is faith simply a choice?

Between Sessions

Personal Reflection

So the other disciples told him, "We have seen the Lord!" But [Thomas] said to them, "Unless I see the nail marks in his hands and put my finger where the nails were, and put my hand into his side, I will not believe."

A week later his disciples were in the house again, and Thomas was with them. Though the doors were locked, Jesus came and stood among them and said, "Peace be with you!" Then he said to Thomas, "Put your finger here; see my hands. Reach out your hand and put it into my side. Stop doubting and believe."

Thomas said to him, "My Lord and my God!" Then Jesus told him, "Because you have seen me, you have believed; blessed are those who have not seen and yet have believed."

(John 20:25 – 29)

1. Are you surprised by the number of examples in the Bible of people who struggled with doubt and faith? Are you in any way relieved to learn that many have wrestled with serious doubt and have come out on the other side? In the book of Jeremiah, God makes a promise: "You will seek me and find me when you seek me with all your heart" (29:13). Do you believe God welcomes your honest questions and doubts?

2. In what way did Jesus honor and address Thomas's doubts? How do you relate to Thomas's need for direct evidence? Jesus may not be with us in the same way he was in Thomas's day, but he did leave us with some convincing evidence. What kind of evidence do we have today and how open are you to weighing that evidence with an open mind and all your heart?

3. In John 20:29 Jesus tells Thomas that in the future there will be those who will not see him, but will yet believe. What does Jesus point out about those people? Can you suspend your disbelief for a moment and begin to imagine the possibility that Jesus may have spoken these words of blessing and promise about *you*? Can you picture a time when, although you have not seen his hands and touched his side, you might also be convinced and conclude, as Thomas did, that Jesus is your Lord and your God?

Personal Reading

Please read the following book content in preparation for session three:

The Case for Faith, Objection #1: Since Evil and Suffering Exist, a Loving God Cannot

SESSION 3

Evil and Suffering, Part 1

Hardships, suffering, heartbreak, man's inhumanity to man—those were my daily diet as a journalist. This wasn't looking at magazine photos from faraway places; this was the grit and pain of life, up close and personal. I've looked into the eyes of a young mother who had just been told that her only daughter had been molested, mutilated, and murdered. I've listened to courtroom testimony describing gruesome horrors that had been perpetrated against innocent victims. I've visited noisy and chaotic prisons, the trash heaps of society; low-budget nursing homes where the elderly languish after being abandoned by their loved ones; pediatric hospital wards where emaciated children fight vainly against the inexorable advance of cancer; and crime-addled inner cities where drug trafficking and drive-by shootings are all too common. Where was God in all this? If he had the power to instantly stop evil and suffering, why did he turn his back? If he loved these people, why didn't he show it by rescuing them? Is this, I wondered, the real reason: because the very presence of such awful, heart-wrenching suffering actually disproves the existence of a good and loving Father?

Lee Strobel, *The Case for Faith*

Watch This!

Video Teaching Segment

Space is provided to take notes on anything that stands out to you.

Discuss This!

1. Lee points out that the number one objection to the Christian faith is: How can there be a loving God with so much pain and suffering in the world? Why do you think this objection is at the top of the list? What about this issue raises objections about God for you?

"If there is no God, why is there so much good? If there is a God, why is there so much evil?"

—St. Augustine

THINK ABOUT THIS!

"We read stories about horrible evils like the Holocaust, the killing fields of Cambodia, the genocide of Rwanda, and the torture chambers of South America — and we can't help but wonder: Where is God? We watch television coverage of earthquakes and hurricanes in which thousands perish, and we wonder: Why didn't God stop it? We read the statistic that one thousand million people in the world lack the basic necessities of life, and we wonder: Why doesn't God care? We may suffer ourselves with persistent pain or aching loss or seemingly hopeless circumstances, and we wonder: Why doesn't God help? If he is loving and if he is all-powerful and if he is good, then surely all of this suffering should not exist. And yet it does."

Lee Strobel

"The fact of suffering undoubtedly constitutes the single greatest challenge to the Christian faith, and has been in every generation. Its distribution and degree appear to be entirely random and therefore unfair. Sensitive spirits ask if it can possibly be reconciled with God's justice and love."

John Stott, theologian

2. Greg Koukl argues that *every* worldview faces the problem of evil and suffering, and the real question is *which* worldview offers the best explanation. Do you agree with Koukl's logic? Why or why not?

THINK ABOUT THIS!

"Either God wants to abolish evil, and cannot; or he can, but does not want to; or he cannot and does not want to. If he wants to, but cannot, he is impotent. If he can, and does not want to, he is wicked. But, if God both can and wants to abolish evil, then how come evil's in the world?"

Epicurus, philosopher

"A loving God could not possibly be the author of the horrors we have been describing — horrors that continue every day, have continued since time began, and will continue as long as life exists. It is an inconceivable tale of suffering and death, and because the tale is fact — is, in truth, the history of the world — it is obvious that there cannot be a loving God."

Charles Templeton

3. Koukl summarizes the issue of good and evil this way: If God is really good he'd want to get rid of all evil in the world, and if he is really powerful he'd be able to, but evil exists; therefore he's either not good or he's not all-powerful. How is it possible to resolve this apparent conflict that God cannot be both good and all-powerful?

4. What does it mean to have moral freedom? Do you agree that people are really morally free creatures? Why or why not? What are some possible reasons why God gave us moral freedom?

5. In the video segment, Rick Warren states that our greatest blessing—the ability to make moral choices—is also our greatest curse. Does Warren's reasoning make sense to you? Why or why not? Give an example.

THINK ABOUT THIS!

"If God is all-powerful, he can do anything. If God is all-good, he wants only what is good. If God is all-wise, he knows what is good. So if all of those beliefs are true — and Christians believe they are — then it would seem that the consequence is that no evil can exist. But evil does exist. Therefore, isn't it logical to assume that such a God doesn't exist?"

Lee Strobel

"What does it mean when we say that God is all-powerful? That means he can do everything that is meaningful, everything that is possible, everything that makes any sense at all. God cannot make himself cease to exist. He cannot make good evil or evil good. Precisely because he is all-powerful, he can't do some things. He can't make mistakes. Only weak and stupid beings make mistakes. One such mistake would be to try to create a self-contradiction, like two plus two equals five or a round square."

Peter Kreeft

6. Do you agree that the source of the world's evil is not God, but rather the result of human freedom and poor human choices? Why or why not? Give examples.

"On my door there's a cartoon of two turtles. One says, 'Sometimes I'd like to ask why he allows poverty, famine, and injustice when he could do something about it.' The other turtle says, 'I'm afraid God might ask me the same question.'"

— Peter Kreeft

THINK ABOUT THIS!

God saw all that he had made, and it was very good. And there was evening, and there was morning — the sixth day.

Genesis 1:31

"This answers the question you hear so often: 'Why didn't God merely create a world where suffering and evil didn't exist?' The answer is: He did. Genesis says that when God created the world, it was 'good.' But if God is not the author of pain or evil or

death, how did they get introduced? Well, God decided to give human beings free will, which is necessary if we are to be able to express love to God and to each other. If you pull the string on a Barbie doll and it says, 'I love you,' that doesn't mean anything because it's been programmed to say it. Real love must involve a choice."

Lee Strobel

"Now, the classic defense of God against the problem of evil is that it's not logically possible to have free will and no possibility of moral evil. In other words, once God chose to create human beings with free will, then it was up to them, rather than to God, as to whether there was sin or not. That's what free will means. Built into the situation of God deciding to create human beings is the chance of evil and, consequently, the suffering that results.

"It's a self-contradiction — a meaningless nothing — to have a world where there's real choice while at the same time no possibility of choosing evil. To ask why God didn't create such a world is like asking why God didn't create colorless color or round squares.

"Then is God the creator of evil? No, he created the possibility of evil; people actualized that potentiality. The source of evil is not God's power but mankind's freedom. Even an all-powerful God could not have created a world in which people had genuine freedom and yet there was no potentiality for sin, because our freedom includes the possibility of sin within its own meaning."

Peter Kreeft

7. What are the negatives and positives of free choice? Overall, was it a good or bad thing to be created with the freedom to choose? Explain. What might a world without moral freedom look like?

THINK ABOUT THIS!

"Why didn't God create a world without human freedom? Because that would have been a world without humans. Would it have been a place without hate? Yes. A place without suffering? Yes. But it also would have been a world without love, which is the highest value in the universe. That highest good never could have been experienced. Real love — our love of God and our love of each other — must involve a choice. But with the granting of that choice comes the possibility that people would choose instead to hate."

Peter Kreeft

8. How is free will related to love? Is free will necessary for love to exist? In what way is the ability to love dependent on free choice? What would forced love look like?

9. Why do you think God didn't just create a world where moral freedom didn't exist in the first place, and in that way, eliminate the potential for human evil and suffering?

THINK ABOUT THIS!

"Pretend you're God and try to create a better world in your imagination. Try to create utopia. But you have to think through the consequences of everything you try to improve. Every time you use force to prevent evil, you take away freedom. To prevent all evil, you must remove all freedom and reduce people to puppets, which means they would then lack the ability to freely choose love."

Peter Kreeft

OPTIONAL DISCUSSION QUESTIONS
for Those Investigating Christianity

• J. P. Moreland and Peter Kreeft point out that even though God is all-powerful, there are some things that God cannot do. For example, God cannot violate the laws of logic or violate his own nature. Do you agree with this logic? Why or why not? How might this line of reasoning shed light on how an all-powerful and good God could allow evil in the world?

• Why do you suppose there is not *more* evil in this world than there already is?

• Christians believe in five things: First, God exists. Second, God is all-good. Third, God is all-powerful. Fourth, God is all-wise. And, fifth, evil exists. How can all those statements be true at the same time?

• If, as J. P. Moreland states, one possible definition of evil is a lack of goodness in the world, how does this tie in with human free will?

• Given the risk that God took in giving humankind free choice, what value do you suppose God placed on humankind's freedom?

• J. P. Moreland says it's possible to have good without evil, but it's not possible to have evil without good. What does Moreland mean? Do you agree or disagree? Why?

• Some argue that God is ultimately responsible for evil because he created humans with free will. What do you think? Is God responsible for evil? Explain.

Between Sessions

Personal Reflection

I have told you these things, so that in me you may have peace. In this world you will have trouble. But take heart! I have overcome the world.

(John 16:33)

Grace and peace to you from God our Father and the Lord Jesus Christ, who gave himself for our sins to rescue us from the present evil age, according to the will of our God and Father.

(Galatians 1:3–4)

1. What is it about pain and suffering that is so abhorrent? Why do we seem to instinctively sense that evil is an aberration and it does not belong in our world? Where do we get the awareness that there should be less evil, rather than more of it? How do we know we are right?

2. Why does human choice result in so much atrocity? Why is evil the logical result of sin? Is this what sin is—free choice gone wild? If God created a perfectly good and just world and sin is defined as rebellion against God, doesn't it follow that sin results in the breakdown of the goodness in the world? Isn't sin the enemy? Do you really believe that?

3. What kind of sin has rocked your world? What kind of sin could you have lived without? Think about your own sin. How many times have you done something you've sincerely regretted that has hurt another person? Have you ever wished you could go back in time and wipe the slate clean?

4. When Jesus told his followers, "Take heart! I have overcome the world," what encouragement was he giving to us all? According to the verses quoted from John and Galatians, how did Jesus overcome the world? And for what cause did he give his life? If Jesus came to give his life for the sins of the world, then why is there still so much evil in it? When will all the pain and hurt be over?

5. Because Jesus took upon himself the consequences for every sin ever committed that has caused you pain, how might this begin to heal you? Because he chose to take the punishment you deserve for every sin you have ever committed, how might this begin to set you free from the weight of guilt and condemnation and replace it with relief, gratitude, and joy?

6. The Bible clearly teaches that to those who receive the gift Jesus offers, there is coming a day of closure—when pain and sin will be forever wiped out. If his death on the cross for our sins can really redeem the world and rescue us from this present evil age, how might this begin to give you peace and hope for the future?

Personal Reading

Please reread the following book content in preparation for session four:

The Case for Faith, Objection #1: Since Evil and Suffering Exist, a Loving God Cannot

Evil and Suffering, Part 2

Jesus acknowledges that because of the acts of humanity that opened the door to evil in this world, we have pain, we have suffering. He doesn't try to cover it up. It's an inevitable part of life. And he tells us something else that's even more important: "I have overcome the world." We have real hope. Hope that's based upon the central doctrine of Christianity — God became a man and entered directly into the suffering of the world.

Lee Strobel, *The Case for Faith*

Watch This!

Video Teaching Segment

Space is provided to take notes on anything that stands out to you.

Discuss This!

1. Do you think God sometimes uses evil and suffering to accomplish a greater good? Explain your answer.

THINK ABOUT THIS!

And we know that God causes all things to work together for good to those who love God, to those who are called according to His purpose.

Romans 8:28 NASB

"Even though suffering isn't good, God can use it to accomplish good. When God accomplishes something positive out of the negatives of life, he fulfills his promise in Romans 8:28, which says God will take the bad circumstances that befall us and cause good to emerge, if we're committed to following him. The Old Testament gives us a great example in the story of Joseph, who went through terrible suffering, being sold into slavery by his brothers, falsely accused, falsely imprisoned. Finally, after a dozen years, he was elevated to a position of great authority, where he could save the lives of his family and many others. And this is what he said to his brothers about his suffering in Genesis 50:20: 'You intended to harm me, but God intended it for good to accomplish what is now being done, the saving of many lives.'"

Lee Strobel

"Since God is the highest good, he would not allow any evil to exist in his works unless his omnipotence and goodness were such as to bring good even out of evil."

St. Augustine

2. Greg Koukl suggests that just as loving parents sometimes allow their children to struggle through difficult things for good reasons, God does the same thing with us. Do you agree or disagree? In what ways might a loving, divine Father sometimes allow short-term pain for long-term gain?

THINK ABOUT THIS!

Consider it pure joy, my brothers and sisters, whenever you face trials of many kinds, because you know that the testing of your faith produces perseverance. Let persever-ance finish its work so that you may be mature and complete, not lacking anything.

James 1:2 – 4

Not only so, but we also glory in our sufferings, because we know that suffering pro-duces perseverance; perseverance, character; and character, hope.

Romans 5:3 – 4

"We know that moral character gets formed through hardship, through overcom-ing obstacles, through enduring despite difficulties. Courage, for example, would be impossible in a world without pain. The apostle Paul testified to this refining qual-ity of suffering when he wrote that 'suffering produces perseverance; perseverance, character; and character, hope.' Let's face it: we learn from the mistakes we make and the suffering they bring. The universe is a soul-making machine, and part of that process is learning, maturing, and growing through difficult and challenging and painful experiences. The point of our lives in this world isn't comfort, but train-ing and preparation for eternity. Scripture tells us that even Jesus 'learned obedience through suffering' — and if that was true for him, why wouldn't it be true for us?"

Peter Kreeft

3. How have difficulties, challenges, and even pain shaped your character and values? How are you different today as a result of the problems you've faced in life? Can you ever imagine thanking God someday for how suffering has molded you? Why or why not?

"God whispers to us in our pleasures, speaks in our conscience,
but shouts in our pains: It is His megaphone to rouse a deaf world."
— C. S. Lewis

4. Joni Eareckson Tada believes that everything God puts his hand to is done with brilliant intention. She says that we can rest assured that although the purposes for suffering might be hidden from us in this present life, God's reasons are always wise, specific, and good. Which points of Tada's do you agree with? Which points do you disagree with? How does one ever come to the place where he or she can trust God so completely? Can you imagine trusting God to this extent?

THINK ABOUT THIS!

What I received I passed on to you as of first importance: that Christ died for our sins according to the Scriptures, that he was buried, that he was raised on the third day according to the Scriptures.

1 Corinthians 15:3 – 4

For Christ also suffered once for sins, the righteous for the unrighteous, to bring you to God. He was put to death in the body but made alive in the Spirit.

1 Peter 3:18

For God so loved the world that he gave his one and only Son, that whoever believes in him shall not perish but have eternal life.

John 3:16

> *"God has demonstrated how the very worst thing that has ever happened in the history of the world ended up resulting in the very best thing that has ever happened in the history of the world. At the time, nobody saw how anything good could ever result from this tragedy — the death of God himself on the cross. And yet God foresaw that the result would be the opening of heaven to human beings. So the worst tragedy in history brought about the most glorious event in history. And if it happened there — if the ultimate evil can result in the ultimate good — it can happen elsewhere, even in our own individual lives. Here, God lifts the curtain and lets us see it. Elsewhere he simply says, 'Trust me.'"*
>
> Peter Kreeft

5. Peter Kreeft contends that the supreme demonstration of God's ability to use suffering and evil for good was revealed in the death of Jesus. Why did God allow Jesus to suffer on the cross? According to Scripture, what ultimate purpose, or greater good, did Jesus accomplish through his death?

"God, if he is all-wise, knows not only the present but the future. And he knows not only present good and evil but future good and evil. If his wisdom vastly exceeds ours, it is at least possible that a loving God could deliberately tolerate horrible things like starvation because he foresees that in the long run that more people will be better and happier than if he miraculously intervened. That's at least intellectually possible."

— Peter Kreeft

THINK ABOUT THIS!

"Jesus said in John 16:33 that in this sinful world, trouble is inevitable. And yet we've all seen examples of how the same suffering that causes one person to turn bitter, to reject God, to become hard and angry and sullen, can cause another person to turn to God, to become more gentle and more loving and more tender, willing to reach out to compassionately help other people who are in pain. Some who lose a child to a drunk driver turn inward in chronic rage and despair; another turns outward to help others by creating Mothers Against Drunk Drivers. One philosopher put it this way: 'I believe all suffering is at least potential good, an opportunity for good. It's up to our free choice to actualize that potential. Not all of us benefit from suffering and learn from it, because that's up to us, it's up to our free will.'"

Lee Strobel

6. As a prisoner in a Nazi concentration camp in 1944, Corrie ten Boom said, "There is no pit so deep that the love of God is not deeper still." Explain what you think she may have meant by these words.

THINK ABOUT THIS!

"Sometimes skeptics scoff at the Bible saying that God can cause good to emerge from our pain if we run toward him instead of away from him. But I've watched it happen in my own life. I've experienced God's goodness through deep pain, and no skeptic can dispute that. The God who the skeptic denies is the same God who held our hands in the deep, dark places; who strengthened our marriage; who deepened our faith; who increased our reliance on him; who gave us two more children; and who infused our lives with new purpose and meaning so that we can make a difference to others."

Marc Harrienger

7. Atheist Bertrand Russell once said, "No one can sit at the bedside of a dying child and still believe in God," yet the tragic death of Marc Harrienger's young daughter drove him toward deeper faith in God. What do you think is the difference between someone who moves further from God in the midst of pain and someone who moves closer to him? What hope could an atheistic worldview bring to a dying child?

8. To what extent do you believe God can really identify with the sufferings of humankind? Assuming the incarnation is true and God took on human flesh, how would that help him relate to the human condition?

THINK ABOUT THIS!

All praise to the God and Father of our Lord Jesus Christ. He is the source of every mercy and the God who comforts us. He comforts us in all our troubles so that we can comfort others. When others are troubled, we will be able to give them the same comfort God has given us.

2 Corinthians 1:3 – 4 NLT

The LORD is close to the brokenhearted; he rescues those who are crushed in spirit.

Psalm 34:18 NLT

"We live in a broken world; Jesus was honest enough to tell us we'd have trials and tribulations. Sure, I'd like to understand more about why. But [Peter] Kreeft's conclusion was right — the ultimate answer is Jesus' presence. That sounds sappy, I know. But just wait — when your world is rocked, you don't want philosophy or theology as much as you want the reality of Christ. He was the answer for me. He was the very answer we needed."

Marc Harrienger

9. Paul points out in 2 Corinthians 4 that compared with eternity, our suffering on earth is "momentary." If you knew for sure that God would one day rid the world of all evil, bring about absolute justice, and usher us into heaven, how might this promise affect your ability to face the trials of today?

THINK ABOUT THIS!

Therefore we do not lose heart. Though outwardly we are wasting away, yet inwardly we are being renewed day by day. For our light and momentary troubles are achieving for us an eternal glory that far outweighs them all. So we fix our eyes not on what is seen, but on what is unseen, since what is seen is temporary, but what is unseen is eternal.

2 Corinthians 4:16 – 18

I consider that our present sufferings are not worth comparing with the glory that will be revealed in us.

Romans 8:18

However, as it is written: "No eye has seen, no ear has heard, no mind has conceived what God has prepared for those who love him"

1 Corinthians 2:9 NIV 1984

Then I saw "a new heaven and a new earth," for the first heaven and the first earth had passed away, and there was no longer any sea. I saw the Holy City, the new Jerusalem, coming down out of heaven from God, prepared as a bride beautifully dressed for her husband. And I heard a loud voice from the throne saying, "Look! God's dwelling place is now among the people, and he will dwell with them. They will be his people, and God himself will be with them and be their God. 'He will wipe every tear from their eyes. There will be no more death' or mourning or crying or pain, for the old order of things has passed away." He who was seated on the throne said, "I am making everything new!"

Revelation 21:1 – 5

The Lord is not slow in keeping his promise, as some understand slowness. Instead he is patient with you, not wanting anyone to perish, but everyone to come to repentance.

2 Peter 3:9

"A lot of times you'll hear people say: 'If God has the power to eradicate evil and suffering, why doesn't he do it?' And the answer is that because he hasn't done it yet doesn't mean he won't do it. In fact, the Bible says that the day will come when sickness and pain will be eradicated and people will be held accountable for the evil they've committed. So what's holding Jesus up? The answer is that some of you are. He's delaying the consummation of history in anticipation that some of you will still put your trust in him. He's delaying everything out of his love for you."

Lee Strobel

OPTIONAL DISCUSSION QUESTIONS
for Those Investigating Christianity

• Peter Kreeft says he believes all suffering contains at least the opportunity for good. Do you agree or disagree? Isn't the idea that God uses evil to make something good somewhat naive or overly simplistic?

• If you were God, how would you have designed the world differently? Would you remove all suffering and evil and tinker with people's free will? What consequences do you surmise would result?

• Second Peter 3:9 refers to the Lord's promise to return to earth and put an end to evil once and for all. What insight does this verse give concerning one reason why God currently tolerates evil?

• How is your view of God affected by the Bible's claim that God entered into the suffering of humankind by becoming a man in Jesus Christ? What is your reaction to the claim that Jesus Christ, out of his great love for you, died on your behalf to pay the penalty for the evil in your life?

• What advantages are there in allowing people to see evil firsthand and then inviting them to reject it in favor of living under God's leadership and goodness?

• If Jesus Christ and his death for you were all God gave you to help you cope with the suffering in your life, could that be enough? Why or why not?

Between Sessions

Personal Reflection

> *He was despised and rejected by mankind, a man of suffering, and familiar with pain. Like one from whom people hide their faces he was despised, and we held him in low esteem. Surely he took up our pain and bore our suffering, yet we considered him punished by God, stricken by him, and afflicted. But he was pierced for our transgressions, he was crushed for our iniquities; the punishment that brought us peace was on him, and by his wounds we are healed. We all, like sheep, have gone astray, each of us has turned to our own way; and the* LORD *has laid on him the iniquity of us all ... Therefore I will give him a portion among the great, and he will divide the spoils with the strong, because he poured out his life unto death, and was numbered with the transgressors. For he bore the sin of many, and made intercession for the transgressors.*
>
> (Isaiah 53:3 – 6, 12)

1. What do you think people mean when they say they have received peace, comfort, or rest from God? Does this seem to be a strange or alien concept to you? To what extent is this a product of overactive imaginations and wishful thinking?

2. Even if God is real, isn't he so far removed from this world that he can't possibly be any comfort to anyone? How can he put his arms around a grieving mother or father? And since he is eternal, how can he even begin to empathize with real human pain or death? Can he possibly understand the frustrations, hurts, and fears of real men and women who have to live with all kinds of evil and suffering in this messed-up world?

3. Exactly how much suffering does the Bible teach God took upon himself? When Jesus took on flesh and blood and entered into the human drama, didn't he experience real human pain? And didn't he somehow, in some kind of divine transaction, take the judgment for *all* the world's suffering and *all* the world's evil for *all time* upon himself? And in so doing, didn't he pay the price for the sins of the whole world?

4. If you could ever begin to believe that Jesus was God in human form, would this be of any comfort to you? If you found that the Bible—God's letter to you—is filled with empathy, love, and a desire to redeem the human condition, would this give you any kind of peace? If, in this same divine book, God promises that one day all suffering will cease and all evil will be eliminated, would this inspire in you any hope for the future? And if you could believe that God comforts those who draw near to him, would you consider inviting him into your life?

Personal Reading

Please read the following book content in preparation for session five:

The Case for Faith, Objection #5: It's Offensive to Claim Jesus Is the Only Way to God

Why Is Jesus
the Only Way to God?

"Fighting words" arouse a visceral response in people, making their guts churn and their hands ball into fists. This offensive language strikes deep inside by attacking their most cherished beliefs, virtually taunting them to lash out in retaliation. To some people, such are the outrageous words of Jesus Christ: "I am the way and the truth and the life. No one comes to the Father except through me." Many people consider it arrogant, narrow-minded, and bigoted for Christians to contend that the only path to God must go through Jesus of Nazareth. In a day of religious pluralism and tolerance, this exclusivity claim is politically incorrect, a verbal slap in the face of other belief systems.

Lee Strobel, *The Case for Faith*

Watch This!

VideoTeaching Segment

Space is provided to take notes on anything that stands out to you.

Discuss This!

1. The apostle Paul stated in Acts 4:12: "Salvation is found in no one else, for there is no other name under heaven given to mankind by which we must be saved." How does this verse strike you? What was your emotional reaction the first time you heard the claim that Jesus is the only path to God? If your viewpoint has changed over time, how has it done so?

THINK ABOUT THIS!

"I am absolutely against any religion that says that one faith is superior to another. I don't see how that is anything different than spiritual racism. It's a way of saying that we are closer to God than you, and that's what leads to hatred."

Rabbi Shmuley Boteach

"Are we to believe only Christians are right? After all ... Christians have the audacity to insist that there is only one God — theirs! And that the gods of every other people on earth are spurious! The apostle Paul stated it bluntly — 'There is no other name under heaven, given among men, by which you may be saved; for there is salvation in no other.' Such an insufferable presumption."

Charles Templeton

"Forgive me for being blunt, but isn't it grossly arrogant for Christians to claim Jesus is the one and only way to God? Why do Christians think they're justified in asserting that they're right and that everybody else in the world is wrong?"

Lee Strobel

2. When he was an atheist, Lee Strobel would often get angry about the blatant arrogance that Christians seemed to display. He would ask, "Who do Christians think they are? Why do they think they can judge everyone else?" What do you think? Do the attitudes of Christians bother you? Why do Christians seem to think they can judge everyone else?

THINK ABOUT THIS!

"If truth is not undergirded by love, it makes the possessor of that truth obnoxious and the truth repulsive. Having been raised in India and having all Hindu, Muslim, Buddhist, and Sikh friends growing up, I can appreciate some of their criticisms of Christians. Christianity's history has some explaining to do with its methodology. Violence, antagonism, and hostility are contrary to the love of Christ. One cannot communicate the love of Christ in non-loving terms. In India we have a proverb that says once you cut off a person's nose, there's no point in giving him a rose to smell. And if a Christian's arrogance turns off somebody, that person won't be receptive to the Christian message. Mahatma Gandhi said, 'I like their Christ, I don't like their Christians.' Friedrich Nietzsche said, 'I will believe in the Redeemer when the Christian looks a little more redeemed.' Their points need to be taken."

Ravi Zacharias

3. Which is more offensive: the message of Christianity or the approach Christians sometimes take to share it? Explain. Describe a time when you were offended by a Christian's attempt to discuss Christianity with you. Describe a time when you were offended by the actual message of Christianity.

"But sometimes it's not the manner in which the Christians try to spread their faith that's offensive. Sometimes people are simply reacting to the message itself."
— Ravi Zacharias

THINK ABOUT THIS!

Jesus answered, "I am the way and the truth and the life. No one comes to the Father except through me. If you really know me, you will know my Father as well. From now on, you do know him and have seen him." Philip said, "Lord, show us the Father and that will be enough for us." Jesus answered: "Don't you know me, Philip, even after I have been among you such a long time? Anyone who has seen me has seen the Father. How can you say, 'Show us the Father'?"

John 14:6 – 9

The high priest said to him, "I charge you under oath by the living God: Tell us if you are the Christ, the Son of God." "Yes, it is as you say," Jesus replied.

Matthew 26:63 – 64 NIV 1984

[Jesus said,] "I and the Father are one."

John 10:30

For just as the Father raises the dead and gives them life, even so the Son gives life to whom he is pleased to give it. Moreover, the Father judges no one, but has entrusted all judgment to the Son, that all may honor the Son just as they honor the Father. Whoever does not honor the Son does not honor the Father, who sent him.

John 5:21 – 23

Then they asked him, "Where is your father?" "You do not know me or my Father," Jesus replied. "If you knew me, you would know my Father also."

John 8:19

[Jesus said,] "Whoever hates me hates my Father as well."

John 15:23

Thomas said to him, "My Lord and my God!" Then Jesus told him, "Because you have seen me, you have believed; blessed are those who have not seen and yet have believed."

John 20:28 – 29

4. Imagine the possibility that Jesus' claims were true and he was in fact God incarnate. Under this circumstance, to what extent do you consider Jesus arrogant for making the statements he did about himself? (See the "Think About This! box on the previous page.) Explain.

5. Jesus' message was deeply offensive to many people, even in his own time. Eleven of the twelve disciples who knew Jesus personally were killed for refusing to renounce what Jesus taught them about himself. In what ways do you think the disciples were arrogant or foolish for continuing to proclaim that they believed Jesus to be the only way to God, even to the point that it got them killed?

6. To what extent have you personally investigated or contemplated one or more of the world religions? Do they teach basically the same thing and thus are there many paths to salvation? What do you find most appealing about these various religions? What most repels you?

FAST FACT

The term "salvation" refers to the process by which fallen human beings can be restored to a right relationship with God. (Christians believe this occurs exclusively through faith in Jesus Christ.)

7. Ravi Zacharias points out that all belief systems make some exclusive claims. Examine the World Religion Comparison chart that follows. Do you agree or disagree that each religion outlined in the chart makes exclusive claims regarding its beliefs? To what extent can all these differing beliefs about God be true at the same time? Explain.

World Religion	Date Started	Founder	Scripture	View of God
Judaism	2000 BC	Abraham (and later Moses, the lawgiver)	The Tanakh (the Old Testament, especially the Torah, or the Law) and the Talmud	Monotheistic; a personal God as revealed in the Tanakh (Old Testament); denies both the Trinity and divinity of Jesus
Hinduism	1800 – 1000 BC	No one founder (developed over many centuries)	The Vedas, Upanishads, Bhagavad Gita	Polytheistic; there are 33 main deities and thousands of lesser gods of which everyone and everything is a part.
Buddhism	525 BC	Siddhartha Gautama (The Buddha or Enlightened One)	The Mahavastu, Tripitaka, Jataka Tales, and the Tantras	Agnostic; Buddha himself did not believe in any gods in particular.

View of Jesus	View of Life After Death	Path to Salvation
Jesus is seen either as a false Messiah, a "good man," a teacher, or he is not considered at all. He did not atone for sins or rise from the dead. Orthodox Jews believe that the Messiah is yet to come.	The orthodox believe in a physical resurrection where the obedient will live forever with God and the unrighteous will suffer.	Prayer, repentance, and obeying the Law (as laid out in the Torah) are necessary for salvation.
Jesus is considered a teacher, a guru, or an avatar (an incarnation of the god Vishnu); he is one of many sons of god. He did not atone for sins or rise from the dead.	Reincarnation to a better status for people who have behaved well and have good *karma* or to a lesser status for those who've behaved poorly and have bad *karma*; the caste system reflects this in that those born into poverty are seen to deserve their low status as a result of past sins.	The goal is to be released from the cycles of reincarnation, which is achieved by knowledge, devotion to a deity, and good deeds (resulting in good *karma*); final salvation is *nirvana*: complete absorption or union with Brahman (the eternal god).
Traditional Buddhism does not address Jesus Christ; Buddhists today generally view Jesus as a good teacher, but not God.	Reincarnation or nirvana; people do not have individual souls or spirits, but one's desires may be reincarnated into another person or creature or cease to exist entirely by attaining *nirvana*.	God is not known to exist; restoration with him is not addressed; there is no such thing as sin; the goal of life is to end suffering by achieving *nirvana*: the end of consciousness by the elimination of all desire; it is achieved by following the eightfold path.

cont.

World Religion	Date Started	Founder	Scripture	View of God
Christianity	AD 30 – 33	Jesus Christ	The Bible (both the Old and New Testaments)	Monotheistic; one personal God in three persons – the Father, the Son, and the Holy Spirit (the Trinity); Jesus (the Son) is God revealed in human form on earth.
Islam	AD 622	Muhammad	The Koran (or the Qu'ran)	Monotheistic; Allah (as revealed by Muhammad in the Koran) is the one true God and cannot be known personally; denies the Trinity and divinity of Jesus.

THINK ABOUT THIS!

"Only someone who doesn't understand the world religions would claim they basically teach the same thing.... In sum, Islam, Buddhism, Hinduism, and Christianity are not saying the same thing. They are distinct and mutually exclusive religious doctrines. They all cannot be true at the same time."

Ravi Zacharias

View of Jesus	View of Life After Death	Path to Salvation
Jesus is God; he exists eternally as the second person of the Trinity. He is the promised Messiah who was prophesied in the Jewish scriptures. He was crucified and physically resurrected, paying the price for human sin and leading the way to forgiveness and eternal life for all who freely choose to believe and follow him.	A human's spirit is eternal and will exist forever either in the presence of the triune God (in heaven) or without him (in hell).	All people are separated from God by sin and the payment for sin is eternal spiritual death and separation from God. Salvation (restoration to God) cannot be earned by human effort but must be received as a free gift of grace found only in the death and resurrection of Jesus Christ.
Jesus was a sinless prophet sent by Allah. He was a great miracle worker but not the Son of God; he was never crucified and killed but miraculously taken alive to "paradise." Some Muslims teach that Jesus will one day return to help convert the world to Islam.	There will be a physical resurrection to eternal torment for infidels and those who do not practice Islam correctly, or eternal pleasure in paradise for those who do.	One's "good deeds" (as defined in the Koran), which includes adherence to the five pillars of Islam, must outweigh the bad; then Allah may grant entrance to paradise. Some Muslims teach that martyrdom for the faith guarantees paradise.

"Even if Ravi Zacharias was right about Christianity, however, does this necessarily mean that all other religions are false? Perhaps they're all teaching the same fundamental truths at their core, using different language, diverse images, and various traditions to communicate basically identical beliefs. Some people say that when you strip away everything, all the world religions are essentially teaching the universal fatherhood of God and the universal brotherhood of humankind. That would mean that all the world's faith systems are equally valid."

Lee Strobel

FAST FACT

The law of non-contradiction is a fundamental principle of thought and logic based on the teaching of Aristotle, which states: "One cannot say of something that it is and that it is not in the same respect and at the same time." In other words, two propositions that contradict one another cannot both be true. They can both be false (leaving room for another possibility), but they cannot both be true.

8. J. P. Moreland states that the world religions could all be wrong, but they can't all be right because they clearly contradict one another. According to this logic (and the law of non-contradiction), can any two of the religions outlined in the chart be true at the same time? Which beliefs about God contradict one another and therefore cannot be true at the same time? Explain.

"Moses could mediate on the law;
Muhammad could brandish a sword;
Buddha could give personal counsel;
Confucius could offer wise sayings; but
none of these men was qualified to offer
an atonement for the sins of the world."
— Theologian R. C. Sproul

THINK ABOUT THIS!

"Buddhism and other religious systems basically tell people how to pull themselves up by their ethical bootstraps. I have never had a problem knowing what is right and wrong in most situations; what I have lacked is the will to do what is right. That's where Christ comes in. He says if you'll bring all of yourself to him, he will not only give you eternal life, but he will change what you want to do in this life."

Ravi Zacharias

Salvation is found in no one else, for there is no other name under heaven given to mankind by which we must be saved.

Acts 4:12

Before long, the world will not see me anymore, but you will see me. Because I live, you also will live. On that day you will realize that I am in my Father, and you are in me, and I am in you. Whoever has my commands and keeps them is the one who loves me. The one who loves me will be loved by my Father, and I too will love them and show myself to them.

John 14:19 – 21

9. Greg Koukl points out that Christianity is the only religion that is entirely lost if you take out its founder. That is because, unlike all other world religions, Christianity is not based on the teachings and rules of Jesus, but on a relationship with the person of Jesus. What do you think it is about Jesus that makes him so different from the other religious founders and so critical to salvation?

THINK ABOUT THIS!

The Christian View of Salvation

Jesus Christ paid the price for our sins and provides a free gift of salvation that cannot be earned by good deeds or human efforts. (Ephesians 2:8 – 9, Titus 3:5)

We must confess and repent (or turn away) from sin. (1 John 1:9)

We must believe and receive God's offer of forgiveness through Jesus Christ. (John 1:12)

OPTIONAL DISCUSSION QUESTIONS
for Those Investigating Christianity

- How likely does it seem to you that any one religion would have the final say regarding truth?

- In what ways do the exclusive claims of Christianity concern, bother, or embarrass you? How might this exclusivity hinder or prevent you from considering becoming a Christian?

- Aren't the world religions really just different roads that lead to the same destination? If we wind up at the same destination, does it even matter how we get there? What is the final destination?

- *If Christianity is true, then all other religions are equally true.* True or false? *If Christianity is true, then all other world religions must be false.* True or false? Explain your answers.

- Refer to the World Religions Comparison chart. What are some of the most surprising or interesting things you learned about the religions listed? What did you learn about Christianity that you didn't already know?

- How do the other world religions compare or contrast with the teaching of salvation in biblical Christianity, as stated in the "Think About This!" box on the previous page?

- Which, if any, religion resonates with you most? Why?

Between Sessions

Personal Reflection

> *Jesus answered, "I am the way and the truth and the life. No one comes to the Father except through me. If you really know me, you will know my Father as well. From now on, you do know him and have seen him."*

> (John 14:6–7)

1. *"I am the way."* What does Jesus mean when he says he's the way? Which way does Jesus take us? It's one thing for him to state he's *the way* to God, but quite another to claim he's the *only way* to God. Does he really think he's the only way? How does this strike you? What is it about the exclusivity of Jesus that most offends people? Is it the claim that followers of other religions have it all wrong? Is it the arrogance of Christians who think they're so much more enlightened than everyone else? Or is this narrow-minded plan simply just too rigid to believe? If Christians are sincerely wrong in believing Jesus to be the one and only way to heaven, why should it bother others who don't believe it? What difference does it make if it's not true? What about you: Do you believe Jesus to be *the* way to God?

2. *"I am the truth."* What does Jesus mean when he says he is *the truth*? Did Jesus really think he was the embodiment of all truth? How could that be possible? Jesus responded to the Roman governor before his crucifixion with the following statement, "The reason I was born and came into the world is to testify to the truth. Everyone on the side of truth listens to me" (John 18:37). Jesus clearly believed himself to be absolutely aligned with truth, and he proclaimed it unapologetically. Pilate himself asked Jesus, "What is truth?" Do you think absolute truth exists, or have you concluded that all truth is relative? And if truth is relative, how do you know if what you believe about truth is absolutely true? Do you ever wish you could know the truth about truth? Do you ever wish you could accept Jesus as the truth?

3. *"I am the life."* What does Jesus mean when he says he is *the life*? Did he think he was the life-giver? What kind of life do you think Jesus offers? Jesus told his followers he came not only to give them life but to give it to them abundantly. What would it mean to have *abundant* life? Throughout his time on earth, Jesus offered people forgiveness for sin, physical and emotional healing, unconditional love, compassion, wisdom, moral

clarity, community, restoration to God, spiritual peace, and eternal life. Which of these things do you long for in your own life? Which of these might you be able to achieve on your own, without God's supernatural intervention? Are you moving toward the place where you would like to receive Jesus' offer of abundant life?

4. Do you sometimes wish you had faith enough to convince you that *only Jesus is the way, the truth, and the life*? Consider asking God to increase your faith right now, just as the disciples once did.

Personal Reading

Please read the following book content in preparation for session six:

The Case for Faith, conclusion: The Power of Faith

The Power of Faith

Throughout my research I was struck by how clearly the Bible defines the spiritual condition of the human race. We're all separated from God by our sin, because he's perfect and pure and holy and we're not. None of us has lived up to our own standard of morality, much less to God's, which is infinitely higher. And because the justice of God is also perfect, our sin should separate us from him for eternity. Among the world's religions, the Christian doctrine of grace is absolutely unique. Grace means that there's nothing we can do ourselves that qualifies us for salvation. Outstanding moral behavior or a lifetime of good works — they're not going to get the job done. That's because God's forgiveness is a gift that we can never deserve and we can never earn.

Lee Strobel, *The Case for Faith*

Watch This!

Video Teaching Segment

Space is provided to take notes on anything that stands out to you.

Discuss This!

1. Do you agree that people in general hunger for purpose and meaning in life? What evidence supports this notion? In what ways do you long for purpose and meaning in your own life?

2. In the video, Craig Hazen states that people in virtually every culture throughout history have sensed they are "not right with the universe" and therefore "not right with God." Do you agree with this claim? Why or why not? To what extent do you feel not right with the universe or not right with God? Explain.

"Jesus Christ didn't come into this world to make bad people good, he came into this world to make dead people live. He came so that those who are dead to God can come alive to God."
— Ravi Zacharias

3. To what degree do you believe that all people are separated and alienated from God? Do you feel close to, or alienated from, God at this point in your life? What do you believe is the cause of your current relational proximity to God?

THINK ABOUT THIS!

For all have sinned and fall short of the glory of God.

Romans 3:23

Your iniquities have separated you from your God; your sins have hidden his face from you, so that he will not hear.

Isaiah 59:2

If we claim to be without sin, we deceive ourselves and the truth is not in us.

1 John 1:8

But God demonstrates his own love for us in this: While we were still sinners, Christ died for us.

Romans 5:8

"Though it's hard to comprehend, the worst thing is to tell God you don't need him. Why? Because a dead person can be restored to life by God; a bereaved person can find peace from God; a person who has been violated can find God's sustenance and strength and even see God conquer through the dark mystery of evil. In other words, there is recourse through these atrocities and tragedies. But to a person who says he or she doesn't need God, what is the recourse? There is none. The question is, 'Have I come to the realization that I've fallen short of God's perfect standard and, therefore, apart from the grace of God, I have no possibility of being with him in heaven?'"

Ravi Zacharias

4. What are the implications, if any, of the fact that God is holy and perfect and we are not? How do you respond to the biblical claim that the sin in your life is so offensive to God that it has spiritually separated you from him?

5. Which of the Bible passages in the "Think About This!" box below most stands out to you? Give a reason for your response. According to these verses, how is it possible for people to bridge the chasm between a holy God and themselves?

THINK ABOUT THIS!

For God so loved the world that he gave his one and only Son, that whoever believes in him shall not perish but have eternal life. For God did not send his Son into the world to condemn the world, but to save the world through him.

John 3:16 – 17

If you declare with your mouth, "Jesus is Lord," and believe in your heart that God raised him from the dead, you will be saved.

Romans 10:9

He was in the world, and though the world was made through him, the world did not recognize him. He came to that which was his own, but his own did not receive him. Yet to all who did receive him, to those who believed in his name, he gave the right to become children of God.

John 1:10 – 12

6. If salvation is a free gift available to all, why do you think not everyone receives it? Why do many people seem to insist on working for their salvation instead of receiving the free gift of grace?

THINK ABOUT THIS!

For it is by grace you have been saved, through faith — and this not from yourselves, it is the gift of God — not by works, so that no one can boast.

Ephesians 2:8 – 9

They asked him, "What must we do to do the works God requires?" Jesus answered, "The work of God is this: to believe in the one he has sent."

John 6:28 – 29

For the wages of sin is death, but the gift of God is eternal life in Christ Jesus our Lord.

Romans 6:23

7. Christianity is the only world religion that offers salvation as a free gift that can't be earned. Is this good news to you or is it news that's too good to be true? Explain.

> *"We [Hindus] accept all religions to be true. The real sin is to call someone else a sinner."*
> — Indian philosopher Swami Vivekananda at the World Parliament of Religions in 1893

8. Read and discuss C. S. Lewis's challenge in the "Think About This!" box on the next page. Do you follow Lewis's logic? Do you agree with his conclusion? Do you think Jesus was a lunatic, a liar, a legend, or the Lord God? Explain.

> *"Anyone can claim to be the only path to God. In fact, quite a few crackpots have made that assertion throughout history. The real issue is why anybody should believe Jesus was telling the truth when he said it."*
> — Lee Strobel

THINK ABOUT THIS!

"A man who was merely a man and said the sort of things Jesus said would not be a great moral teacher. He would either be a lunatic ... or else he would be the Devil of Hell. You must make your choice. Either this man was, and is, the Son of God; or else a madman or something worse. You can shut Him up for a fool, you can spit at Him and you kill Him as a demon, or you can fall at His feet and call Him Lord and God. But let us not come with any patronizing nonsense about His being a great human teacher. He has not left that open to us. He did not intend to."

C. S. Lewis, *Mere Christianity*

9. N. T. Wright points out that the resurrection of Jesus proves that nobody else but Jesus Christ has led the way through death and out the other side. If this is true, what implications are there for those who believe and trust Christ? What impact would this make on your life personally?

THINK ABOUT THIS!

"Billy Graham once told of meeting Konrad Adenauer, the mayor of Cologne who was imprisoned by Hitler for opposing the Nazi regime and who later became the highly regarded chancellor of West Germany from 1949 to 1963. Adenauer looked Graham in the eyes and asked, 'Do you believe in the resurrection of Jesus Christ from the dead?' Graham said, 'Of course I do.' To which Adenauer replied: 'Mr. Graham, outside of the resurrection of Jesus, I do not know of any other hope for this world.' He was right. Because the resurrection is an actual historical event, we can be forgiven, we can be reconciled with God, we can spend eternity with him, and we can trust Jesus' teachings as being from God. You can say that the resurrection of Jesus established him as being the son of God. If that's true, then all other faith systems cannot be true, because they each assert something contrary to his divinity."

Ravi Zacharias

OPTIONAL DISCUSSION QUESTIONS
for Those Investigating Christianity

• How do you define sin? What are the repercussions of sin, if any? Are you a sinner? Why or why not?

• According to the Bible, Jesus Christ is the only one who solved the sin problem, which is why he is the only way to God. Do you see any other way to solve the sin problem?

• What are the various ways in which people insist on earning forgiveness or attempt to fix their sin problem by their own efforts?

• In what way is Jesus' resurrection proof of his ability to keep his promises to forgive sin and grant eternal life?

• What difference does it make to you personally that Jesus Christ came into the world, lived a perfect life, died on the cross for your sins, and rose again?

• If Jesus really is the only way to God, how would wholeheartedly believing that make a difference in your life?

In the Coming Days

Personal Reflection

> *Jesus said to them, "Very truly I tell you, it is not Moses who has given you the bread from heaven, but it is my Father who gives you the true bread from heaven. For the bread of God is the bread that comes down from heaven and gives life to the world." "Sir," they said, "always give us this bread." Then Jesus declared, "I am the bread of life. Whoever comes to me will never go hungry, and whoever believes in me will never be thirsty."*
>
> (John 6:32–35)

> *Jesus answered, "Everyone who drinks this water will be thirsty again, but whoever drinks the water I give them will never thirst. Indeed, the water I give them will become in them a spring of water welling up to eternal life.*
>
> (John 4:13–14)

1. Christianity has been defined as, "One beggar telling another beggar where to find bread." Christians are sinners who were living in rebellion against God but found forgiveness and grace through Jesus Christ. And now they just want to pass this discovery of new life on to the rest of the world. Do you personally believe this is the intention of most Christians? More importantly, do you believe this was the intention of Jesus Christ?

2. Jesus once described himself metaphorically as "the bread of life," and he taught that those who come to him will never again hunger and those who believe in him will never again thirst. How important is bread and water to survival? What do you think Jesus intended to convey by comparing himself to such basic sustenance?

3. Do you ever find yourself in need of being spiritually filled? What does it feel like to be spiritually hungry or even spiritually depleted? How do you think it would feel to be filled in such a way as never to hunger or thirst this way again? Do you believe that this is even possible?

4. The Bible gives a challenge to those of us who don't yet know God personally and invites us to: "Taste and see that the Lord is good!" You have probably never concluded you didn't like a particular food without tasting it first. If we "taste" what Jesus has to offer, and if we honestly ingest him into our lives—our decisions, our fears, and our failures—he promises to give us his peace, his presence, and his rest. Jesus once said, "Come to Me, all who are weary and heavy-laden, and I will give you rest" (Matthew 11:28 NASB). Is your soul weary and wishing for peace? Is your soul heavy and hungry for rest? If you find yourself longing to be filled, why not pray right now and ask Jesus to forgive your sins and to sustain your life? Why not taste of the bread of life and the living water that is offered freely to you even at this very moment?

Small Group Leader Helps

To ensure a successful small group experience, read the following information before beginning.

Group Preparation

Whether your small group has been meeting together for years or is gathering for the first time, be sure to designate a consistent time and place to work through the six sessions. Once you establish the when and where of your times together, select a facilitator who will keep discussions on track and an eye on the clock. If you choose to rotate this responsibility, assign the six sessions to their respective facilitators up front, so that group members can prepare their thoughts and questions prior to the session they are responsible for leading. Follow the same assignment procedure should your group want to serve any snacks or beverages.

A Note to Facilitators

As facilitator, you are responsible for honoring the agreed-upon time frame of each meeting, for prompting helpful discussion among your group, and for keeping the dialogue equitable by drawing out quieter members and helping more talkative members to remember that others' insights are valued in your group.

You might find it helpful to preview each session's video teaching segment and then scan the discussion questions that pertain to it, highlighting various questions that you want to be sure to cover during your group's meeting. Ask God in advance of your time together to guide your group's discussion, and then be sensitive to the direction he wishes to lead.

Urge participants to bring their study guide, pen, and a Bible to every gathering. Encourage them to consider buying a copy of *The Case for Faith* book by Lee Strobel to supplement this study.

Session Format

Each session of the study guide includes the following group components:

- **Watch This!** — Space is provided for individual notes and insights as the group views the session's video presentation, about 30 minutes.

- **Discuss This!** — Video-related and Bible exploration questions reinforce the session content and elicit personal input from every group member. The boxed content ("Think About This!" and "Fast Fact") interspersed throughout this section bears directly on surrounding questions. Either have group members read this content to themselves, read it aloud yourself, or have group members take turns reading it aloud. The latter two options will take longer.

- **Optional Discussion Questions for Those Investigating Christianity** — At the end of the main discussion section are further questions for groups that have more time or interest. You may even choose to substitute a question or two for questions in the main discussion section.

Additionally, in each session you will find a **Between Sessions** section (**In the Coming Days** after session six) that includes suggestions for personal reflection and response as well as recommended reading from *The Case for Faith* book in preparation for the next session.

The Case for Faith

A Journalist Investigates
the Toughest Objections
to Christianity

Lee Strobel
New York Times *Bestselling Author*

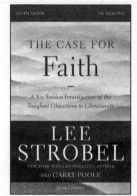

Was God telling the truth when he said,
"You will seek me and find me when you seek
me with all your heart"?

In his #1 bestseller *The Case for Christ*, Lee Strobel examined the
claims of Christ, reaching the hard-won verdict that Jesus is God's
unique son. In *The Case for Faith*, Strobel turns his skills to the most
persistent emotional objections to belief — the eight "heart barriers"
to faith. This Gold Medallion-winning book is for those who may be
feeling attracted to Jesus but who are faced with difficult questions
standing squarely in their path. For Christians, it will deepen their
convictions and give them fresh confidence in discussing Christianity
with even their most skeptical friends.

> "Everyone — seekers, doubters, fervent believers — benefits when Lee
> Strobel hits the road in search of answers, as he does again in The
> Case for Faith. In the course of his probing interviews, some of the
> toughest intellectual obstacles to faith fall away."
>
> Luis Palau

> "Lee Strobel has given believers and skeptics alike a gift in this book.
> He does not avoid seeking the most difficult questions imaginable, and
> refuses to provide simplistic answers that do more harm than good."
>
> Jerry Sittser, professor of religion, Whitworth College, and
> author of A Grace Disguised and The Will of God as a Way of Life

Available in stores and online!

ZONDERVAN®
.com

The Case for Christ: A DVD Study

Investigating the Evidence
for Jesus

Lee Strobel and Garry Poole

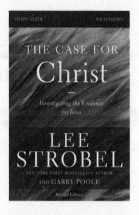

Is there credible evidence that Jesus of
Nazareth really is the Son of God?

Skeptics dismiss the Jesus of the Gospels
by claiming there is no evidence in the case for Christ. Lee Strobel
disagrees. The former legal journalist and one-time atheist knows
how to ask tough questions. His own search for truth about Jesus
led him to faith in Christ.

Now Strobel invites you and your group to investigate the truth
about Jesus Christ leading to the facts that guided Strobel from
atheism to faith in Christ. In this revised six-session video with separate study guide, participants will journey along with Strobel on a
quest for the truth about Jesus. Rejecting easy answers, you will sift
through fascinating historical evidence as you weigh compelling ex-
pert testimony. In the end, groups may very well see Jesus in a new
way—and even, like Strobel, find their lives transformed.

The six sessions include:
- The Investigation of a Lifetime
- Eyewitness Evidence
- Evidence Outside the Bible
- Analyzing Jesus
- Evidence for the Resurrection
- Reaching Your Verdict

Available in stores and online!

The Case for Christ for Kids Curriculum

Investigating the Truth about Jesus

Lee Strobel with Christopher D. Hudson

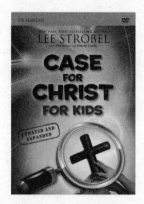

How would the kids in your children's ministry answer friends who ask questions like: Was Jesus really born in a stable? Did his friends tell the truth? Did he really come back from the dead?

In these six lessons children will learn answers to these and other pressing questions in kid-friendly language that will help them grow in their faith. Packed full of well-researched, reliable, and fun investigations of some of the biggest questions kids have, *The Case for Christ for Kids Curriculum* brings Jesus to life by addressing the existence, miracles, ministry, and resurrection of Christ.

This DVD-ROM makes your children's ministry planning simple and includes everything you need for a successful Sunday school, children's church, or VBS program:
- A checklist to help leaders organize each week's study
- Lesson Plans
- Family Pages
- Promotional materials
- AND a VBS expansion kit to help leaders teach *The Case for Christ for Kids Curriculum* as a Vacation Bible School or Backyard Bible Club program

The six sessions include:
- The Case of the Promised Baby
- The Case of the Voice from Heaven
- The Case of the Eyewitnesses
- The Case of the Wedding Crisis
- The Case of the Living Water
- The Case of the Risen Jesus

Available in stores and online!

ZONDERVAN®
.com

The Case for a Creator: A DVD Study

Investigating the Scientific Evidence That Points toward God

Lee Strobel and Garry Poole

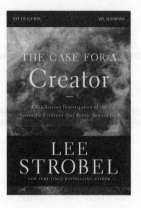

"My road to atheism was paved by science . . . But, ironically, so was my later journey to God." – **Lee Strobel**

Former atheist Lee Strobel has discovered that science, far from being the enemy of faith, now provides a solid foundation for belief in God. New scientific discoveries point to the incredible complexity of our universe, a complexity best explained by the existence of a Creator.

This revised six-session video and separate study guide invites participants to encounter this evidence delivered in a compelling conversational style. Join Strobel in reexamining the theories that once led him away from God. Pastors and small group leaders seeking resources that answer tough questions about the existence of God will find compelling answers in *The Case for a Creator: A DVD Study*.

The six sessions include:
- Science and God
- Doubts about Darwinism
- The Evidence of Cosmology
- The Fine-tuning of the Universe
- The Evidence of Biochemistry
- DNA and the Origin of Life

Available in stores and online!

Faith Under Fire: A DVD Study

Exploring Christianity's Ten Toughest Questions

Lee Strobel and Garry Poole

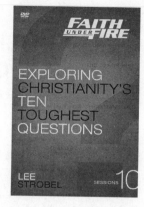

Faith Under Fire is a ten-session small group Bible study exploring Christianity's toughest questions, including the existence of God, Christianity and Islam, the reliability of the Bible, and faith and science. On the video, bestselling author Lee Strobel hosts spirited discussions between well-respected Christians, people of other faiths, and people with no faith at all, on the some of the most important spiritual and social issues of our time. The participant's guide will help you and your group sift through and gain understanding on these controversial and relevant issues that surround the Christian faith and many of its most pertinent cultural issues. Strobel provides additional comments to guide small group discussion.

Sessions include:

1. Is the Supernatural Real?
2. Is Jesus a Prophet or the Son of God?
3. Did Jesus Rise from the Dead?
4. Do All Roads Lead to God?
5. Is the Bible Bogus?
6. Does Science Point to a Creator?
7. Is Anything Beyond Forgiveness?
8. Why Does God Allow Pain and Suffering?
9. The Mystery of the Trinity?
10. Do Christians and Muslims Worship the Same God?

Available in stores and online!

ZONDERVAN®
.com

Becoming a Contagious Christian Participant's Guide

Communicating Your Faith in a Style That Fits You

Mark Mittelberg, Lee Strobel, and Bill Hybels

Releasing the hidden evangelist in every Christian—

Becoming a Contagious Christian is a proven course designed to equip believers for effective evangelism in today's world. It avoids stereotyped approaches that feel intimidating to many Christians. Instead, it shows ordinary believers how they can share the gospel in a natural and powerful way while being the person God made them to be.

Each session's exercises, discussions, self-assessments, and video vignettes give step-by-step guidance to help participants become effective communicators for Christ to those around them. Used with nearly 1 million people, *Becoming a Contagious Christian* is an innovative and unparalleled program for training Christians in relational evangelism.

Becoming a Contagious Christian works with any size group, from small groups of 4-9 to Sunday school classes and other large groups of 10 to 150 or more. It can be presented successfully in any of the following formats: three sessions of two hours each; six sessions of 50 minutes each; one, two, or three-day retreats. Or adapt it to fit the needs of your church!

Sessions include:
1. The Benefits of Becoming a Contagious Christian
2. Being Yourself—and Impacting Others
3. Deepening Your Relationships and Conversations
4. Telling Your Story
5. Communicating God's Message
6. Helping Your Friends Cross the Line of Faith

Available in stores and online!